A JUNGLE … E FABLE

Donkey Wisdom

Paul White

A JUNGLE DOCTOR PICTURE FABLE

Donkey Wisdom

10 Publishing
a division of 10 of those.com

This edition published in Great Britain in 2017

Reprinted 2018, 2021

British Library Cataloguing in Publication Data
A record for this book is available from the British Library

ISBN: 978-1-911272-24-3

Designed and typeset by Pete Barnsley (CreativeHoot.com)
Illustrations by Peter Oram

Printed in China

Cover text - 'A_Font_with_Serifs' and inside text - 'Kiddish'

10Publishing, a division of 10ofthose.com
Unit C, Tomlinson Road, Leyland, PR25 2DY, England

Email: info@10ofthose.com
Website: www.10ofthose.com

A JUNGLE DOCTOR PICTURE FABLE

Donkey Wisdom

Punda, the donkey, was unhappy. "It isn't fair," he said. "Simba, the lion, has beautiful tawny skin. Twiga, the giraffe, is golden and mottled like the sunlight and shadow under thorn trees. But I'm just black."

"What's wrong with that?" said Toto, the monkey. "It doesn't show the dirt, does it, Hippo?"

Boohoo, the hippo, shook his head. "And - um - it's useful. On dark nights lions and leopards can't see you."

Donkey sighed. "How I wish I could change my colour!"

"There's one place in the jungle where wishes come true," smiled Toto.

Boohoo mumbled, "I don't - um - think you should tell him. It's spooky and if he goes there - um ..."

"His wish might come true," chuckled Toto.

"Where is it?" demanded Punda. "Tell me. Where do wishes come true?"

"It's a magic cave," said Toto.

"Then come on. Let's go."

"Um, do you think it's wise?" asked Boohoo.

"Of course it isn't," said Toto shivering, "but it could be an adventure."

"Then please take me," begged Punda. "If wishes come true, I wish I was white. Wouldn't it be wonderful to be a dazzling, white donkey?"

"Oh dear," panted Boohoo. "It's a long way. My poor feet are ..."

"Stop grumbling," shouted Toto. "There's the cave. In you go, Punda, and start wishing."

Donkey's voice trembled. "It looks dark in there."

"Yes," said Boohoo. "Dark and clammy - um - there's still time to change your mind."

"Oh shush," chuckled Toto. "Keep quiet, Boohoo. Punda is big enough to take care of himself. Donkey, do you or don't you want to be white?"

"Yes, I do," said Punda. "I do. I do."

"Then come to the cave and make a wish."

"Let's all go together," said Punda, his teeth chattering.

"Um - but I haven't any wishes to make, none at all," chuckled Boohoo. "And Toto, if you went into that cave and heard creepy noises, you'd - um - turn white before he would."

Toto sniffed. "You're very brave, outside the cave. Eh, that's poetry."

"Stop making all that noise," breathed Donkey. "I'm going in."

After they had waited a long minute, Boohoo said, "You shouldn't have told him about this cave. You have a big mouth."

Toto's eyes stuck out. "Look who's talking. You could eat a whole watermelon sideways."

"Look at me," came Punda's voice loudly.

"Um - eh - ooh?" gulped Hippo.

Monkey jumped up and down. "He's white. Donkey's really white, white! Hey! How did you change colour, Punda?"

"I went into the dark cave and I called out, 'I wish I was white.' And now I am. I'm the only white donkey in the jungle. Do you like my new colour, Toto?"

"It'll show the dirt. You'll never keep it clean."

"I'll be very careful," said Punda hopefully.

"Mm," mused Toto. "But you won't stay white for long. You'll be a sort of dirty grey. That's the best of being black. It doesn't show the dirt."

"Oh dear," said Punda. "For a while the others will admire me, but when I look grey and grubby they'll laugh. I wish I was black again."

"Where's he going?" asked Boohoo.

"Back to the cave to wish again. He seems to want to be black," said Toto.

"He does have - um - trouble making up his mind, doesn't he?" replied Hippo. "And it's all your fault, you muddle-headed monkey. You brought us all the way for nothing. You ought to be - eh - ooh, what's that?"

"Toto! Boohoo!" shouted Donkey. "Look, I'm back again and black again."

"Um," nodded Boohoo. "That's the donkey we know. What a – um – beautiful, black beast."

Punda tossed his head. "I'm glad you like it. Black's a good colour, don't you think, Toto?"

"Yes, but it's very common."

"What do you mean?" demanded Donkey.

"Well," said Toto, scratching his head, "Every donkey you see is black. If you want to stand out you have to be different."

Punda stamped his feet. "But you said ..."

"I know, I know," nodded Toto. "That was before I had time to think about it. You were quite right. Black is dull and not very attractive."

Donkey was most upset. "Then I'll go back and wish again."

Toto shouted, "I'll come with you."

"Can I come too?" asked Boohoo.

Toto laughed. "I don't think you'll ever come too."

"Ohh." Boohoo's voice sounded boomy and strange. "It's dark."

"Hullo," shouted Toto. The echo came back: H-U-L-L-O!

"Don't d-d-do that," said Boohoo. "You'll wake up the spooks!"

"Punda, start wishing quickly – ooh! What's that?" said Toto.

"You walked right into me," said Donkey.

"Well, it's so dark and you're so black!"

"As I said before," mumbled Boohoo, "black is a good colour when you don't want lions to see you at night."

"But I want to be white," shouted Punda.

"That's very dangerous," said Hippo, shaking his head.

"Oh," gulped Donkey. "Then I wish I was black."

"Then you'd be just like any other donkey," sniffed Toto.

"Oh dear," yelled Donkey. "Then I wish I was white ... or black ... no, white; that is, black."

The echo came back: Black! White! Black! White!

Suddenly there was a vast rumbling. "What's happening?" gulped Hippo.

"Quickly," shouted Toto. "The roof's falling in. Let's get out, O-U-T!"

Hippo sneezed. "Hipp, hipp, hipp - oschoo!"

"Please," said Toto. "Please mind where you're blowing."

"Sorry," snorted Boohoo. "Dust always makes me sneeze and wheeze!"

"What about my fur?" retorted Toto. "Dirt all over me."

"Ha ha ha ha," laughed Toto.

"Ho ho ho ho," chuckled Boohoo.

"What's so funny?" demanded Donkey.

"Ha ha, you're black and white, and you're white and black – ho ho – and black and white, ha ha!"

"Oh NO!" groaned Punda. "I've stripes all over me. I must wish again."

"It's too late. The cave fell in just as we got out," grinned Toto.

Punda shook his head. "Oh, why can't I make up my mind?"

Now you know what a zebra is - a donkey who can't make up his mind.

The most important thing you can do is to decide to ask Jesus to forgive your sin and to give you everlasting life.

Read about it in John's Gospel,
chapter 3, verse 16 and
Romans, chapter 10, verses
9, 10 and 11.

The
Jungle
Doctor

Paul White was born in Bowral, Australia.

As a doctor in Tanganyika, Paul learned a great deal from his African friends at the jungle hospital. They befriended him and helped him in his efforts to learn their language, Chigogo.

One of their most important gifts was to teach him how to use animal stories. These stories, or fables, help to explain different elements of Christian life.

The first of six fable books appeared in 1955. In these books you will meet Toto, the mischievous monkey; Boohoo, the Hippo who, like the author, suffered from allergies; Twiga, the giraffe and wise teacher; and many others.

We hope these animals will endear themselves to you.

THE JUNGLE DOCTOR PICTURE FABLE SERIES ...

AVAILABLE FROM 10OFTHOSE.COM

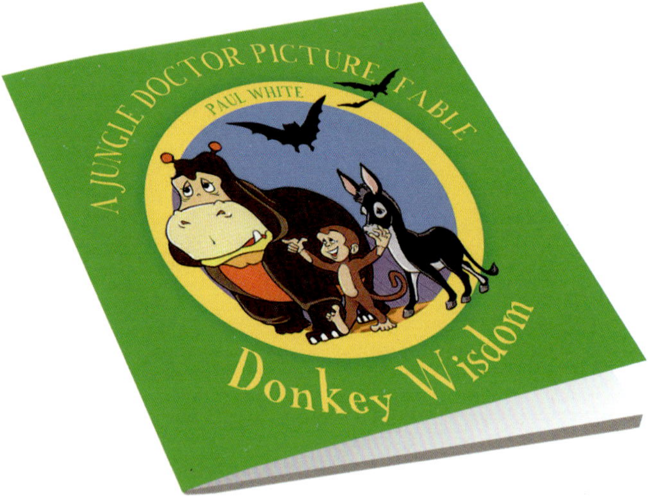
A JUNGLE DOCTOR PICTURE FABLE
PAUL WHITE
Donkey Wisdom